What Would You Call...?

(Clean, Humorous Riddles That Can Usually Be Solved With a Pun)

by Tam S. Hutchinson, Jr.

ISBN: 0-578-17146-5
ISBN-13: 978-0-578-17146-3
Library of Congress Control Number: 2015917235
AJEST Publishing, North Wilkesboro, North Carolina

Published by AJEST Publishing
a division of Chick Haven Feed Service, Inc.
www.ajestpublishing.com
Book design and illustrations by Marie Finkhousen

Printed in the United States of America
2015

Dedication

To my family: Karen, Andrew, Joseph, Evan, Stephen and Timothy—for their encouragement, inspiration, and suggestions.

Acknowledgements

Joseph compiled much of the first draft from years of my notes.

Karen and Evan each contributed one of the riddles.

Allison Lyall helped me get started with the illustration ideas. Marie Finkhousen offered several illustration ideas, handled the illustrations, and did the cover art.

All of my family reviewed the manuscript and provided feedback.

Mr. Edward W Rilee, Esquire, of MacCord Mason in Greensboro, NC, provided legal advice on portions of the text.

6

About the Author

I am an erstwhile poultry farmer, computer programmer, and community college math instructor. I am married to the wonderful Karen Hutchinson. We have five super sons: Andrew, Joseph, Evan, Stephen, and Timothy (hence, the name of the publishing company). The whole family contributed to this book in many ways. I love to laugh. Proverbs 17:22 (KJV) says, "A merry heart doeth good like a medicine: but a broken spirit drieth the bones." I trust that this book will bring some additional laughter and joy into your life.

TSH

What did they say about the man who had gone beyond the drops on the grass?

"He was past dew (past due)."

Of what conqueror do you think when you hear your engine running smoothly?

Attila the Hum (Atilla the Hun).

What would you call the dessert that prosecuting attorneys like to eat before they enter the courtroom?

CULP-cakes (cupcakes).

What did the lady say when she had finished making her pickles?

"It's a done dill (It's a done deal)."

What do you call someone who doesn't hold himself or herself up correctly?

An im-POSTURE (an imposter).

What did the nose say to the perfume bottle?

"Odor please (order please)."

Which flavor is never on time?

Choc-o-LATE (chocolate).

What is the highest job title a fellow can have?

Wor-KING Man (working man).

What do you call a maiden who is leader of her tribe?

Miss CHIEF (mischief).

What do you call it when a person is growing beans on the very back of his or her vehicle?

A bumper crop.

What kind of dessert does James Bond prefer?

Spies' cake (spice cake).

What do you call St. Nick out for a joy ride at night?

Santa cruise (Santa Cruz).

What could you call being married
to a domineering woman?

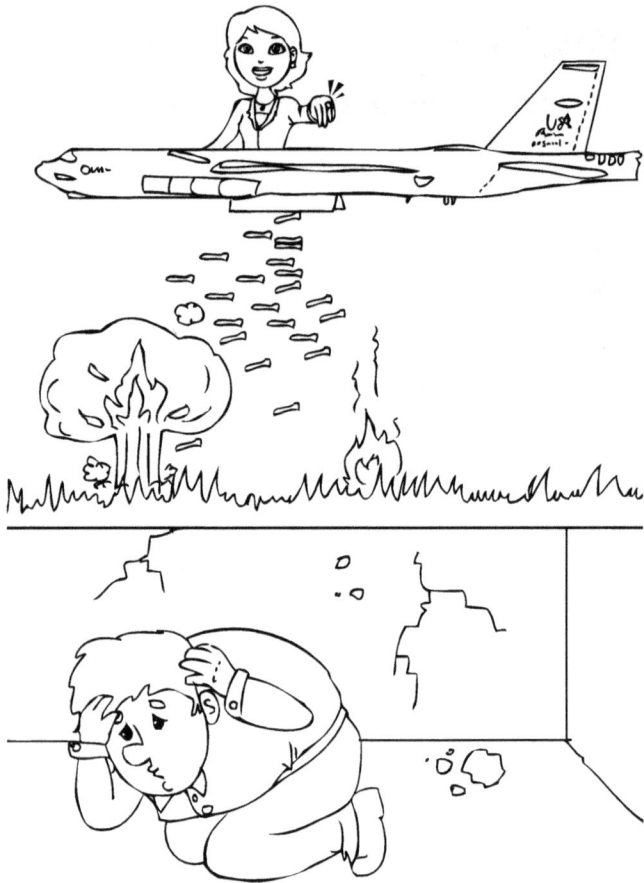

Marital blitz (marital bliss).

What do you call it when fellows climb up into vegetation and create fine particles in the air?

TREE-MEN-DUST (Tremendous).

What could people feel like they need after they have done something wrong?

Peanuts (penance).

How would two people be related if they use bad language at each other?

Cussings (cousins).

What do you call it when believers fight?

Christian friction (Christian fiction).

What misleading answer could one give when asked for the completion date on final adjustments requested for the electronics project?

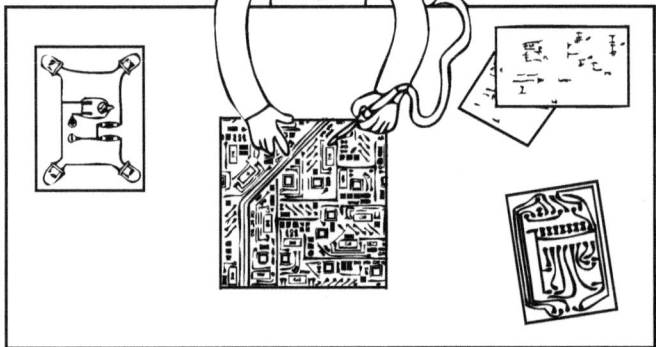

Next tweak (next week).

What do you call a person that does The Twist on the beach?

A SHORE dancer (a short answer).

What do you call a good-natured little fellow who lives under a bridge?

A sweet TROLL (a sweet roll).

What do you call it when you put people who have just eaten into the line-up?

Playing the filled (playing the field).

What do you call a rancher who also has another job?

Farmer-worker (former worker).

What do you call a person who is constantly asking for his Lipton's drink to be refilled?

Tea nagger (teenager).

What do you call an immaculate green vegetable?

A clean bean.

What could you say about people who start walking off in a strange and unusual manner?

"Wierd they go (Where'd they go?)."

Who are the best-looking people in the legal profession?

Pros-e-CUTE-ers (prosecutors).

What could you call a dessert that you cannot eat?

Abstract tart (abstract art).

What do you call a person who is not sure about being not sure?

Empty doubt (emptied out).

What would you call Soviet jets that follow narrow paths in the grass?

Trail Migs (trail mix).

What do you call an online criminal who has been incarcerated?

E-con (econ or economics).

What do you call unhappy, large pieces of ice floating in the ocean?

Angry bergs (Angry Birds™).

What would you call two people who sang together in Alaska?

Yukon duet (you can do it).

What do you call a girl who talks a lot?

Miss Communication
(miscommunication).

What would you call a class in which no one wanted to learn anything?

Interest-free.

What do you call a person who is good at games of chance?

Wizard of odds (Wizard of Oz).

What do you call a mail carrier who is doing some excavation?

Postal digger (post hole digger).

What do you call a relative of a feathered egg-layer?

Chicken's kin (chicken skin).

What could you oddly enough call your eyes when they are red and hurting?

EAR-itated (irritated).

What could you call a slightly overweight relative?

PLUMP-kin (pumpkin).

What do you call it when you have bees all over the world?

Global swarming (Global Warming).

What could you call it when the company twisted around quickly?

Corporate twirled (corporate world).

What could you call an unhappy female sibling of your parents?

Cross AUNT (croissant).

What do you call it when people who are puffing on cigarettes make fun of others?

Smokers' SCOFF (smoker's cough).

How do you tell when a heating/air conditioning person is ready for action?

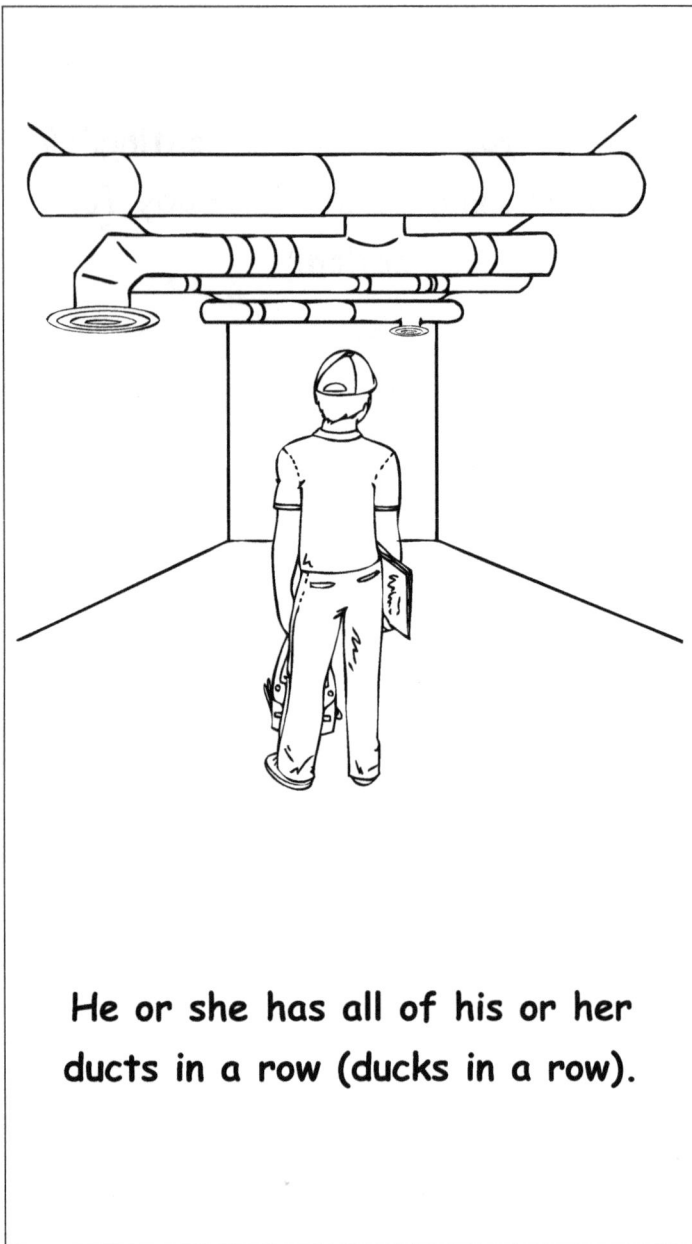

He or she has all of his or her ducts in a row (ducks in a row).

What do you call it when a person doesn't eat much plastic?

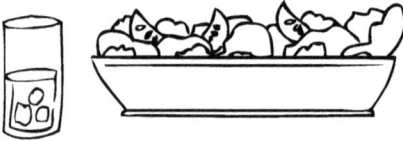

A low-CARD diet (low-carb diet).

What would you call a blazer with many sleeves?

A coat of arms.

What could you call turning one's back to discourage a fellow?

DETER-gent (detergent).

What do you call a drying cloth that is nearby?

A nigh TOWEL (a night owl).

What do you call the guy who is the best at making plays on words?

Pun-KING (punkin' or pumpkin).

What do you call those who favor giving examinations?

Pro-TESTERS (protestors).

What would you call the kind of musical instrument Bill Clinton would play if he were in a field?

Bush-saxe (bush axe).

What excuse did the spice man give for being late?

"I had to change cloves (clothes)."

What do you call a mystery dish served at the beginning of the meal, which contained Macintosh?

Apple TEASER (appetizer).

What could we call it when we had
given Dexter something to eat?

Fed Dex (Fed Ex).

What would you call it if someone fired at dirty clothes?

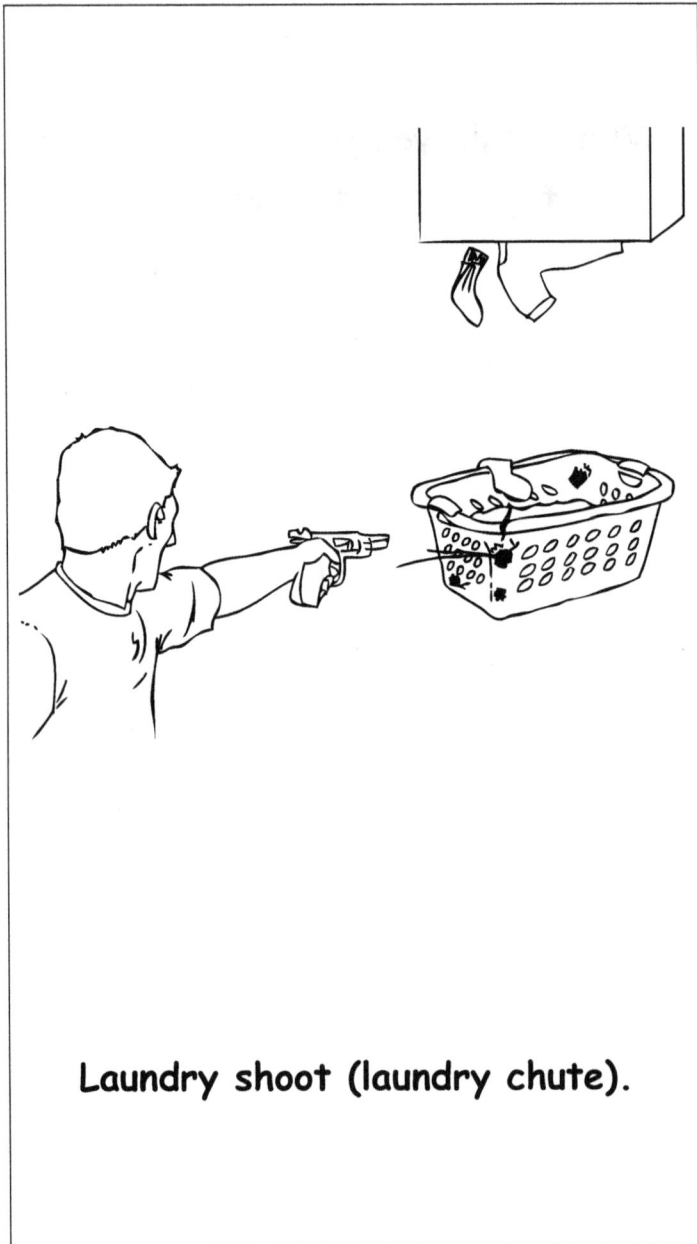

Laundry shoot (laundry chute).

What could you call a business that cuts grass at local financial institutions?

Mowing the banks.

What do you call it when someone laps up his or her booze?

Alcohol-LICK (Alcoholic).

What would you call an arts center in New Mexico with all the color removed from it?

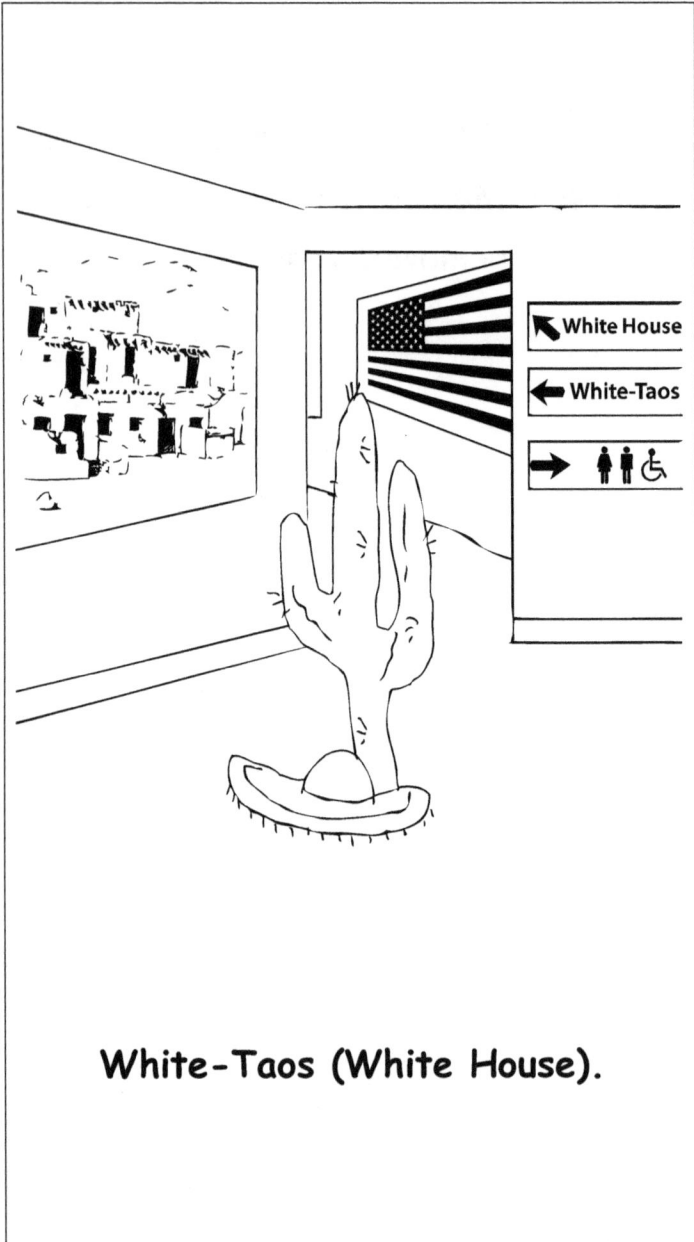

White-Taos (White House).

What would you call it if a construction worker demonstrated his or her jackhammer for the audience?

A rock buster performance (a block buster performance).

What would you call a crocodile in a tuxedo?

Classy crock (classic rock).

What would you call it when the pig's husband spoke?

Boar said (Boar's Head).

What do you call it when someone moves his or her yams around with a broom?

Sweep potatoes (sweet potatoes).

In what country do they like to cut the grass on the hills?

Mow-zem-banks (Mozambique).

How could you describe an artist's rendering of a medieval soldier in battle?

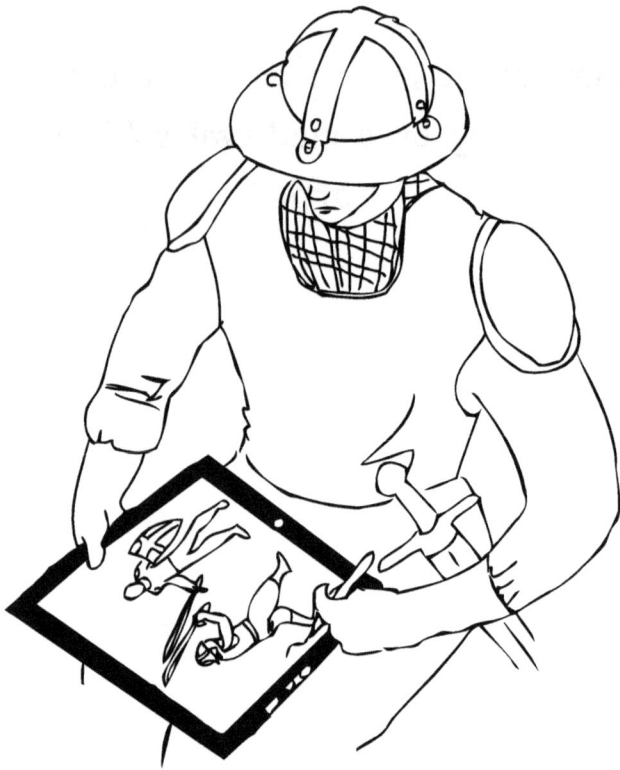

A warrior with drawn sword.

What would you call it if you were on Twitter™ and found an unusually splendid comment?

A rare Tweet (a rare treat).

What do you call a yard in which everything is neatly arranged?

Lawn order (Law and Order).

Where were photos first taken?

In the olym-PICS (Olympics).

What could you call a soldier upon whom the most practical jokes were played?

Top pranked (top ranked).

What would you call tart candy that people eat while sitting at their desks?

Office sours (office hours).

In what famous European city do they always use tops on their cups?

STRAWS-burg (Strasbourg).

What could you say if you liked the taste of your food?

"The spice is right (The Price is Right)."

What kind of blood do most people have in Taiwan?

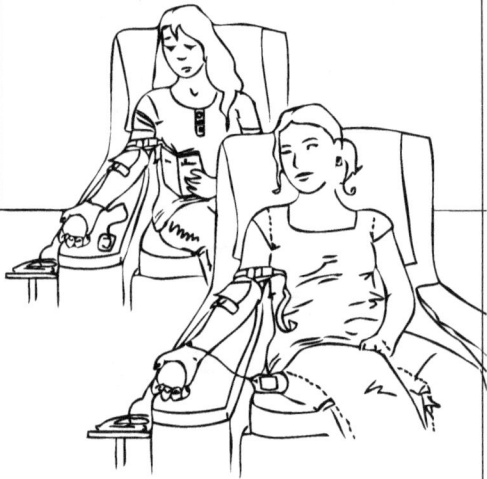

Type A (Taipei).

What was King Arthur's favorite TV program?

Knightly News (Nightly News).

What could you say about a person who has trouble starting fires?

"He or she has a burning disability
(a learning disability)."

What do you call funny cyclists?

Biking hoots (hiking boots).

What could you call it when people worry about losing the farm?

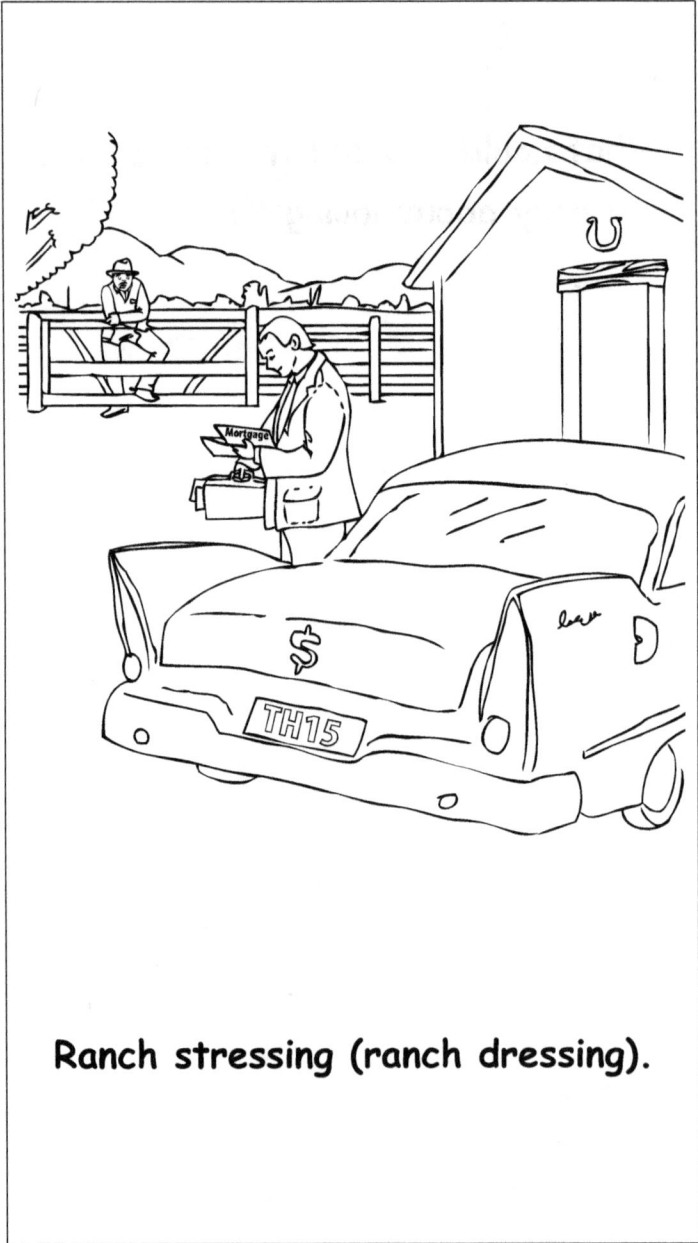

Ranch stressing (ranch dressing).

What do you call it when someone follows a garbage truck around?

A trash stalker (a trash talker).

What type of movie would it be if it were cold?

Refriger-rated (refrigerated).

What could you call it if animal feet grew out of your head?

Mental paws (menopause).

What would you call it if you had a large pickle?

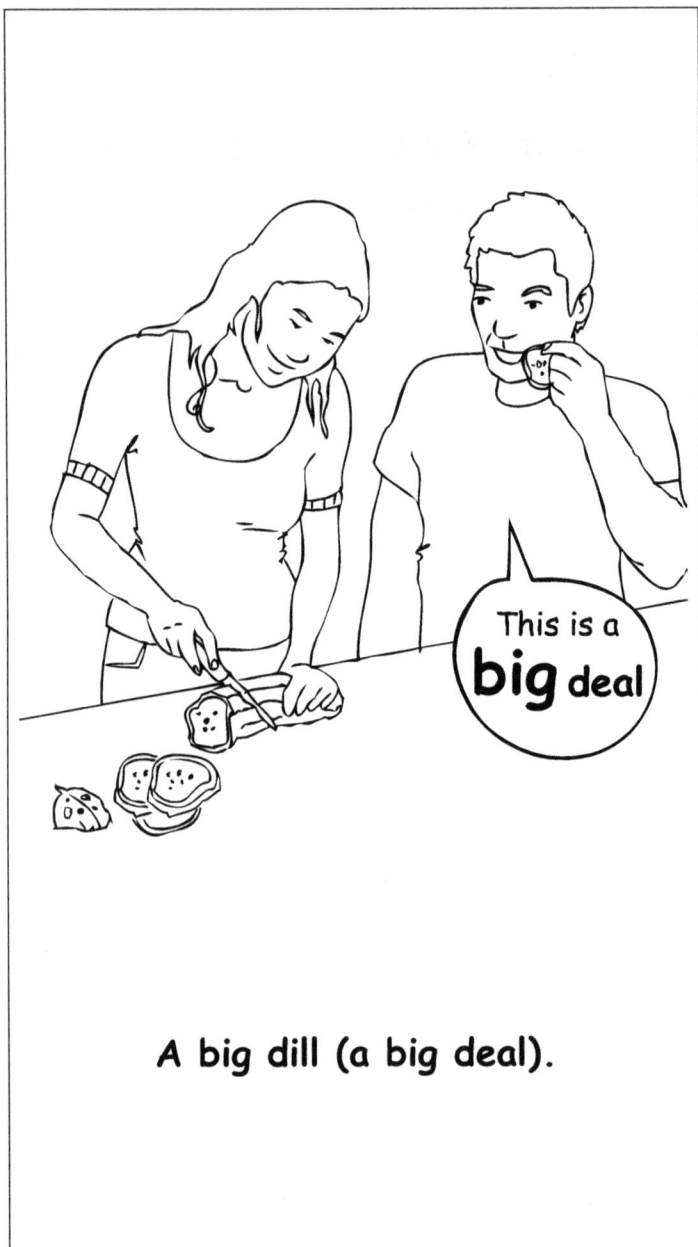

A big dill (a big deal).

What would you call the proven idea that large financial institutions are better than small ones?

Big bank theory (Big Bang Theory).

The length of which internal organ contributes most to longevity?

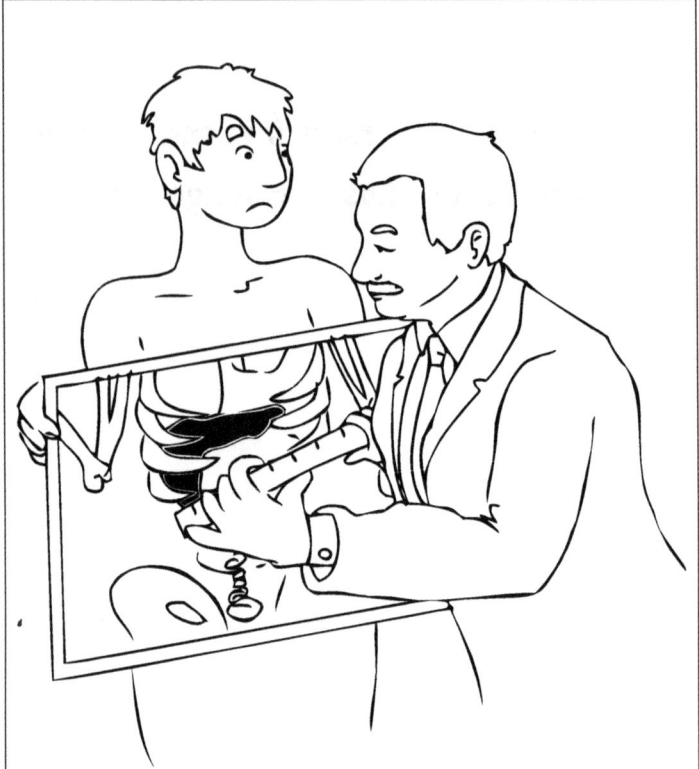

Liver (long liver).

What did one skydiver say to another after a jump?

"Did you have a nice lunge? (lunch)."

What could you say about a young person who could no longer fit into his or her clothes?

Grew some (gruesome).

What could you say about a young person who could no longer fit into his or her clothes?

Grew some (gruesome).

What would you call the best looking photos?

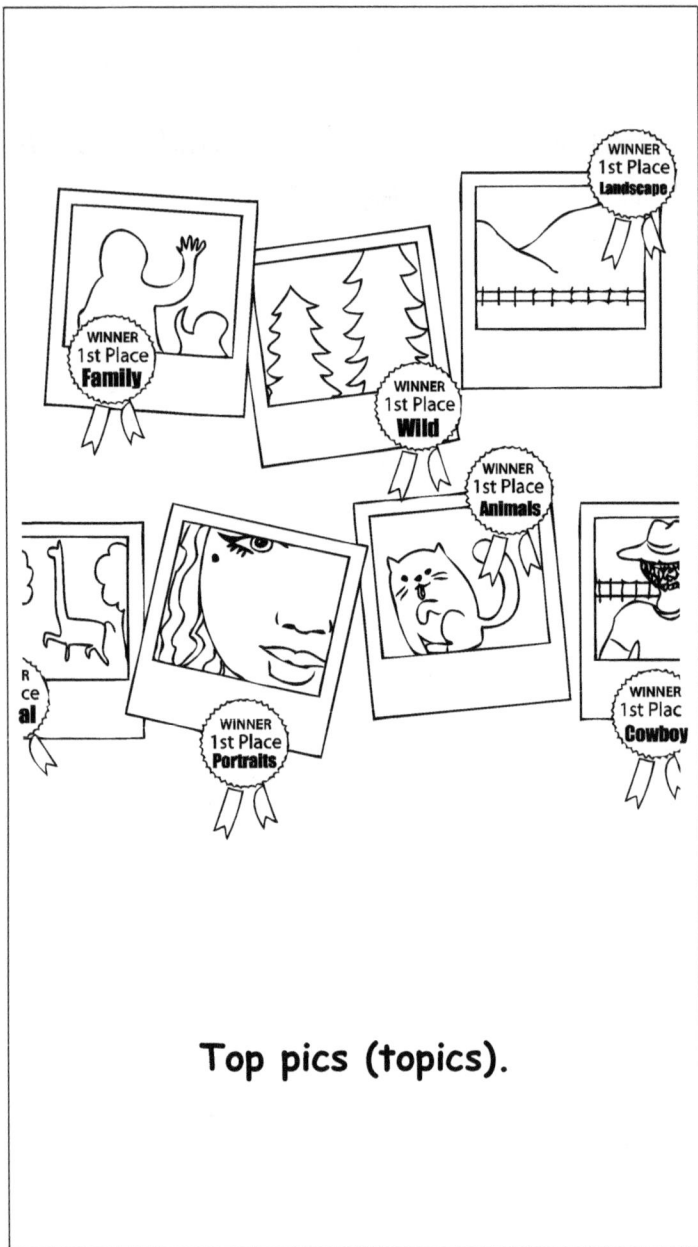

Top pics (topics).

What do you call a person who is tired of winter precipitation?

Snow-bored (snowboard).

What would you call it if someone misspelled a smell?

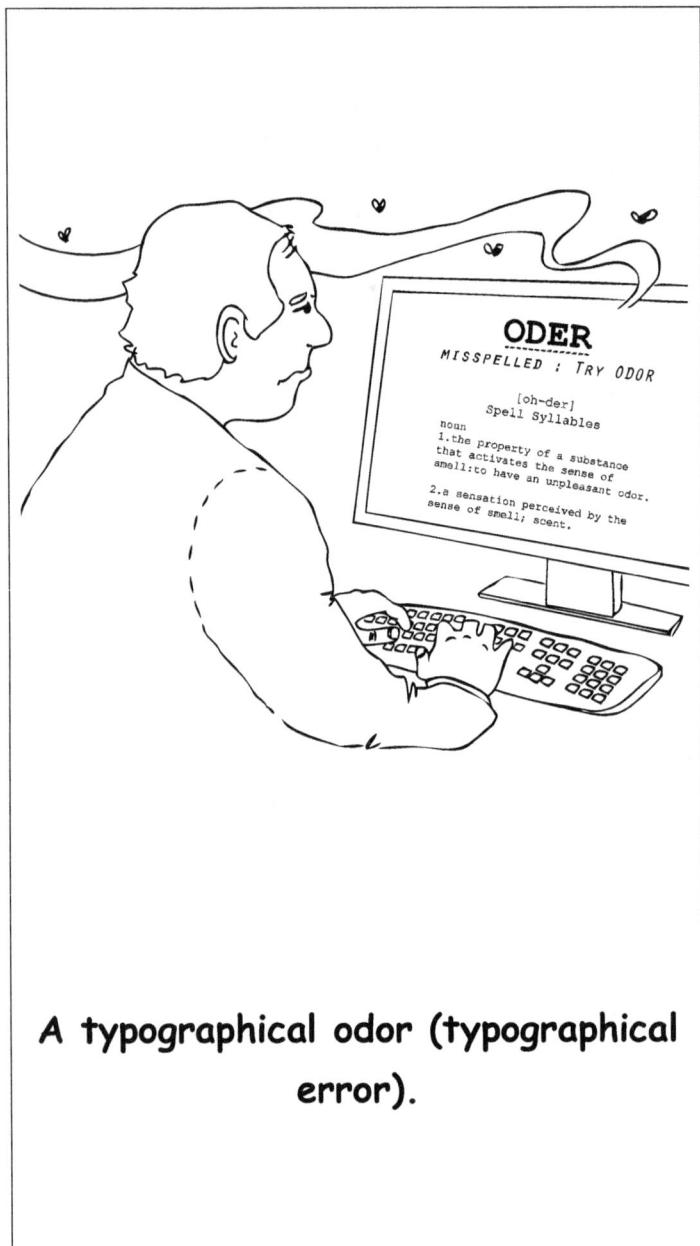

A typographical odor (typographical error).

What would have been a good name for a satellite channel of Bach's day?

The Fugue Network (Food
Network^{SM}).

What would you call it if someone referred to his or her glasses during a presentation?

An optical allusion (optical illusion).

What could you generically call a young girl who did very well in the class?

Maiden A (made an "A").

What dessert do they serve prisoners in France before putting them in the electric chair?

SHOCK-a-lot cake (chocolate cake).

What would you call it when someone got sick from eating a pickle?

Food-borne DILL-ness (food-borne illness).

What would you call the place where the Pope stands to deliver speeches?

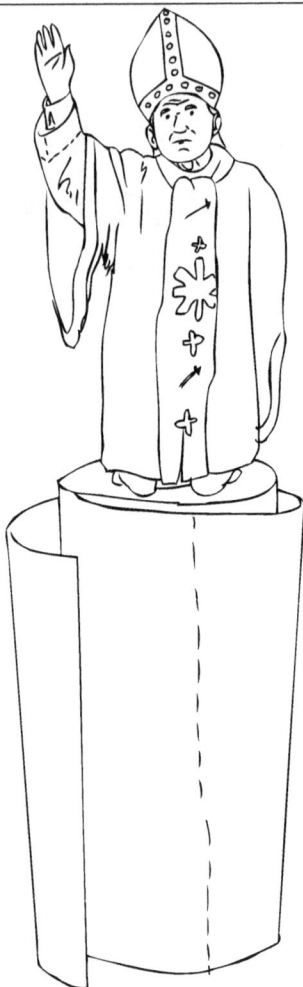

The Papal Tower (paper towel).

What would you call a person who posed as one who took care of sheep, but really was a collector of information about people?

Shepherd-spy (shepherd's pie).

What would you call a meeting to discuss the procedures for withdrawing from a class?

Drop Forum (drop form).

What would you call a person who liked to talk about other people while drinking coffee?

Gos-SIP (gossip).

What would you call a person who designs yards full of vehicles?

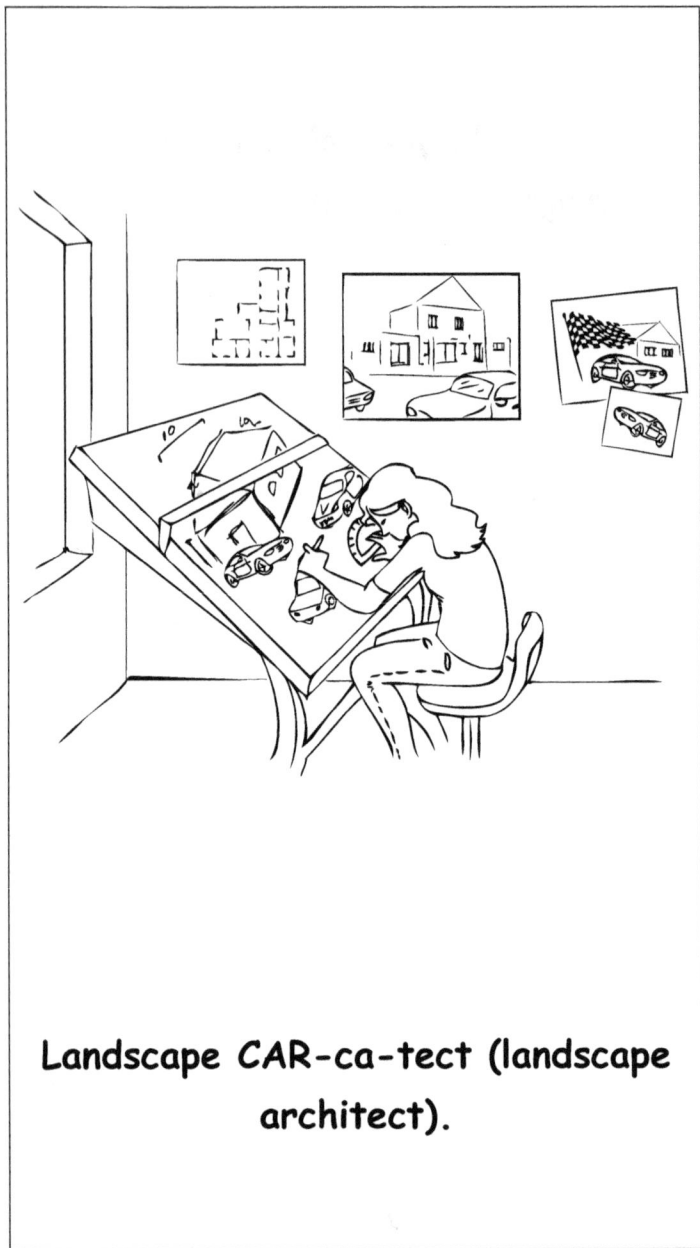

Landscape CAR-ca-tect (landscape architect).

How did the word "pie" originate when a child indicated that he wanted something from the top shelf of the refrigerator?

"It's up high (It's a pie)."

What kind of fruit should one eat before taking a short sleep in the afternoon?

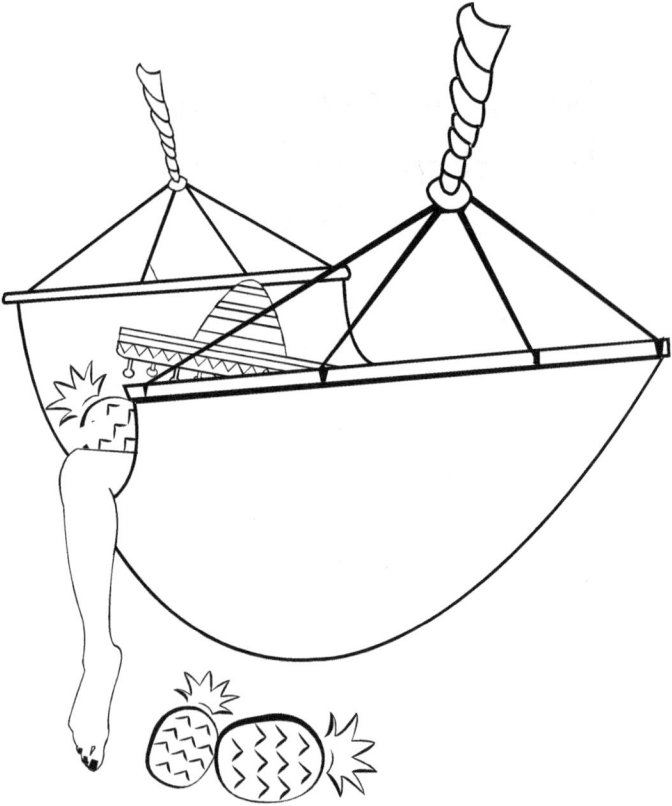

Pine-NAP-ple (pineapple).

What do you call a doctor who calls on patients in the stars and planets?

Cos-medic (cosmetic)

www.ingramcontent.com/pod-product-compliance
Lightning Source LLC
Chambersburg PA
CBHW060921040426
42445CB00011B/736